Zigzagging in the Pacific

My service as an officer on two ammunition ships of the United States Navy in the Pacific during World War II

By Harold J. Cook

For ordering information please contact:
Evangel Author Services
PO Box 189
Nappanee, IN 46550
1-800-253-9315
sales@evangelpublishing.com

Cover design by Mark Burford, Evangel Press

ISBN-13: 978-0-692-00427-2
Library of Congress Control Number: 2009936658

Printed by Evangel Press, Nappanee, Indiana
in the United States of America

Ship on front cover: *USS Pyro* (AE1)

CONTENTS

DEDICATION

To my wife, Dolly, and my three daughters, Nancy, Becky and Sally, for their help and support.

PREFACE

This book is a memoir of my service in the United States Navy during World War II. To refresh my memory, I had three sources of information. First of all, I secured a copy of the ship's log for each of the ships on which I served for the time I was aboard. On my second ship the preparation of the ship's log was part of my duty as the Navigator. Secondly, Commander William F. Lally, the captain of my second ship, at the end of the war had submitted to the Department of the Navy a brief history of the ship. The Department of the Navy sent me a copy of this history. And lastly, I referred to the letters I had written home during the war. My mother had kept all of them intact. Due to censoring we were not allowed to write about where we were or what we were doing, but several of the narratives come from those letters.

In cases where I have used quotation marks, the phrase or words may not be exactly as stated, but the expression is similar to what was said. Otherwise, I believe that all names, dates, events, and stories are basically correct.

Harold J. Cook

CHAPTER 1

"NINETY DAY BLUNDERS"

April 6, 1945 is a day none of the men aboard the USS Las Vegas Victory will ever forget. At 3:20 PM we went to General Quarters— all men at their stations—on notice from SOPA (Senior Officer Present Afloat). As navigator I was on the bridge of the ship, serving as Officer of the Deck with the Captain at my side.

Every pair of eyes remained locked on the horizon, using binoculars to scan for danger. We saw one Japanese plane in flames fall from the clouds. Then we saw a second plane in flames, which was being followed by three fighter planes, crash into the sea.

We spotted another Japanese plane flying about twenty to thirty feet above the water and heading directly toward our ship at a distance of about three miles. We fired, and the plane swerved about 45 degrees to the right and crashed into an LST (landing ship, tank).

It appeared that our ship was the target.

I had the unusual experience of serving as an officer on two United States ammunition ships in the Pacific during World War II. Before I relate that story, I need to tell you about my early days in the United States Navy.

I had graduated from DePauw University, Greencastle, Indiana, in June 1940. At the time of the Japanese attack at Pearl Harbor, I was 23 years old, living in my hometown, Mishawaka, Indiana, and was handling personnel and payroll at the Empire Box Company, located in the neighboring city of South Bend, Indiana.

On Sunday, December 7, 1941, when I heard over the radio about the attack on Pearl Harbor, I did not know what to do. I walked down to the nearby Cline's Drug Store. Other fellows in the neighborhood started drifting in, one by one. We wanted to see somebody, drink a coke—and talk.

The nation was united in patriotism, and all of the enlisting offices were being rushed by men volunteering for the service. Dick Albert, a good friend, and I decided to go to Chicago to sign up for the Navy. For the physical examination, a group of us took off our clothes and a number was painted on each of our chests. Then we had to walk past several doctors. When the doctors saw the high arches on my feet, they immediately signaled that I had failed. Dick passed the physical examination. He later became an officer in the Navy, serving in Iceland during the first part of the war and then later in Hawaii.

I was frustrated and did some checking around. I learned that the Navy had a program called V-7, which was open to college graduates between the ages of 20 and 28, inclusive. The V-7 program was a fifteen-week training course that prepared one to be an officer. Hence, in March 1942, I went to Indianapolis, Indiana, and signed up for the V-7 program. I was given a physical examination by an Indianapolis physician, and this time I passed. I received orders to report to the U.S. Naval Reserve Midshipman School at Columbia University, New York City, on October 26, 1942.

During my first four weeks in the Navy, I lived in John Jay Hall on the Columbia University campus. Then, for the next four weeks I was aboard the *USS Prairie State*, a training ship beached on the mud at 135th Street and the Hudson River. This ship was formerly the battleship *USS Illinois*, pride of the Navy during the years at the beginning of the twentieth century. It had been a part of the great White Fleet that President Theodore Roosevelt had sent around the world. After the four weeks on the *Prairie State*, I went back to John Jay Hall for the rest of my training.

After being apprentice seamen during our first three weeks, we took our oath as midshipmen on November 17, 1942. One of the first things we had to do was learn the Navy language. Floors were now decks, walls were bulkheads, windows were ports. We did not wash the ceiling or the floor. We scrubbed the overhead and swabbed the deck. We did not go to the toilet. We went to the head.

I had a room with a roommate on the ninth floor of John Jay Hall. All of the men in midshipmen school had graduated from college in recent years, and we came from all parts of the United States. The men on the ninth floor were a fun-loving bunch of guys. After a long day of classes and study, we would gather in the hallway for some stories and jokes.

Our day began at 6:10 AM and ended at 10:00 PM when "Taps" was played. The bugler always jazzed it up at the end, and while lying in our bunks we gave him a big hand. We got plenty of exercise—marching drills, gun drills, and rowing whaleboats on the Hudson River. We actually did our marching in the streets of New York. Frequently we had to march under a viaduct with hundreds of pigeons perched above us. As we approached the viaduct, the platoon commander would give the order "double time." We would run under the viaduct, but even then our dark blue uniforms would always get splattered with droppings from the pigeons.

At Midshipmen's School, Columbia University, New York City.
(First man, second row)

We had courses in navigation, ordnance, engineering and damage control, seamanship, and communications. Each day we had four hours of classes and about six hours of study.

If not assigned to a weekend watch, we had weekend liberty. Usually we headed for Times Square. Due to the war, all the lights on the street at night were out or dimmed. All cars and buses were traveling with dimmed lights, and theater marquees and advertising displays were dark. However, the streets were crowded with people, many being military personnel.

One Saturday afternoon when we had liberty, I told my roommate that I would meet him at a certain time in front of one of the theaters near Times Square. I had arrived a little early, and I was standing in front of the theater waiting for him. I was wearing my dark blue midshipman uniform and cap. A woman came up to me and asked where the ladies' powder room was located. When I told her that I did not know, she gave me a disapproving look, turned around, and walked away. Next, a man stepped up and wanted to know how to get to the nearest subway. The questions kept coming—"What's the lowest price seat?" or "When does the main feature start?" I soon realized that they thought that I was a doorman connected with the theater. I quickly solved the problem by stepping off to the side of the theater to wait for my friend.

After three months of classes and study, we took our final exams. Graduation exercises were held on February 17, 1943, at the beautiful Riverside Church near the Columbia University campus. We took the oath as Ensigns—1,270 of us. At that time this was the largest group of officers ever to be sworn in at one time in the history of the United States Navy. Due to the fact that we became officers after three months as midshipmen, we were known as the "Ninety Day Wonders." However, I heard that behind our backs we were jokingly called the "Ninety Day Blunders."

Since the Navy had given each of us new Ensigns a clothing allowance, I went to a store in New York City and purchased a dark blue uniform, a white uniform, some khaki uniforms, and a bridge coat, which is a heavy, dark blue overcoat. Next on the agenda was getting our first assignment. I received orders to report aboard the

USS Pyro (AE-1) somewhere in the South Pacific. I was to report to San Francisco to await a ship that would take me to the *Pyro*.

When I picked up my orders I knew that the AE designation meant ammunition ship. Many of my classmates had received assignments to battleships, cruisers, destroyers, and aircraft carriers. My roommate had received assignment to a destroyer. Several of my classmates stopped by our room to express their sympathy for my being assigned to an ammo ship—"Sorry, Cookie." I jokingly told them, "Hey, whenever you guys run out of ammo, just stop by." Little did I realize that this would become true. Six weeks later I was aboard the *Pyro* which was transferring ammunition to combat ships in the South Pacific

I had a couple of days at home on my way to the West Coast. It was an emotional goodbye to my parents, especially to my father. He was 76 years of age and in poor health.

Upon arriving at San Francisco on March 1, I checked in at the Central Y.M.C.A. on Golden Gate Avenue with my daily rental fee being one dollar. While staying at the Y.M.C.A., I met several young officers who had already served aboard ships in the South Pacific. When they saw my wardrobe, they laughed and advised me that I would not need the heavy bridge coat or the dress white uniform in the South Pacific. Taking their advice I shipped them back to my home in Indiana.

The streets of San Francisco were crowded with sailors and soldiers, but mostly sailors. After a week in San Francisco I received orders to report aboard the *USS Rochambeau* (AP-63) for transportation to the *Pyro*. The *Rochambeau* had been built by the French as *Maréchal Joffre* in 1933. Manned by the Free French after the fall of France in 1940, the ship was in the Philippines when the United States entered World War II. After the receipt of the news from Pearl Harbor, she headed for San Francisco. She was taken over by the U.S. Maritime Commission and transferred to the United States Navy. The ship was named in honor of General Rochambeau, who, with the 5,500-man force he brought with him from France, joined with Washington in the campaign of 1781 against Cornwallis' forces at Yorktown [1]

Aboard the *Rochambeau* I shared a cabin with three other Ensigns, each of us headed to a different ship. Two of them had been classmates at Columbia University. For the next three weeks we played a lot of gin rummy and did a lot of reading. For exercise we would go up to the top deck and toss a medicine ball around. A medicine ball is a large leather ball about three times larger than a basketball. Instead of air it is filled with padding and is heavy. We would toss it back and forth, and it would keep our muscles in good shape. We also did a lot of "sack duty," resting up for what lay ahead of us.

On March 29, 1943, we arrived at Espiritu Santo, the largest of the New Hebrides Islands, which are located in the southwest Pacific about one thousand miles northwest of the Queensland coast of Australia and southeast of the Solomon Islands. At that time the New Hebrides Islands were under joint rule by the British and French governments. My ship, the *Pyro*, was anchored in the large harbor at Espiritu Santo, and I reported aboard that afternoon.

CHAPTER 2

THE OVERLOADED
LIFE RAFT

The keel for the *Pyro* had been laid down on August 9, 1918, at the Pugent Sound Navy Yard, Bremerton, Washington. She was commissioned three years later, being the original ammunition ship of the United States Fleet.[2] "Pyro" is the Greek word for fire. She had a sister ship, the *USS Nitro* (AE-2), which was operating in the Atlantic theater during the first part of World War II. Then during the latter part of the war, the *Nitro* was also in the Pacific.

The *Pyro* had been moored at the West Loch in Pearl Harbor on December 7, 1941, when the Japanese made their historic attack. One bomb landed on the dock within ten feet of the ship's side. Fortunately, the bomb did not set off the ammunition in the holds of the ship or the ammunition stacked on the dock and did not cause any major damage. The *Pyro* was credited with damaging one enemy plane. As a new officer on the ship, I had to listen to the story about the *Pyro* at Pearl Harbor innumerable times.

The *Pyro* had a tonnage of 7,000 pounds, a length of 463 feet, and a beam (width) of 61 feet. At the time I went aboard, the armament consisted of two five-inch guns and two three-inch guns on the stern, two three-inch guns on the bow, and two 1.1 pom-pom guns, one on each side. The top speed was 13 knots, being about 15 miles per hour.

The ammunition was carried in five separate compartments, known as holds. Each hold had an access opening to the deck, known as a hatch, and each hatch had a steel cover.

While anchored at Espiritu Santo the *Pyro* was serving as the primary ammunition ship for the combat ships of the Third Fleet in the area. At that time the Third Fleet was involved in many battles in the nearby Solomon Islands. Between battles the majority of the combat ships came to Espiritu Santo to replenish their depleted supply of ammunition.

The ship had 21 officers and 268 enlisted men. The Captain was a four-striper, Captain Robert L. Boller. Often during our stay at Espiritu Santo, he was the Senior Officer Present Afloat, commonly referred to as S.O.P.A. The Executive Officer was Commander Michael Toal, who had spent many years at sea. We were happy to have on board an M.D., Lieutenant Commander A.A. Norconk, whom we all called "Doc." He also served as the Head Censor. The officers wore khaki uniforms without ties, and the crew wore dungarees, being blue cotton work clothes, and sailor hats.

The *Pyro* was anchored in a berth six or seven miles from the nearest ship. Cruisers, destroyers, and patrol craft would tie up alongside us, and we would transfer the ammunition directly to them. However, for the larger ships, such as the battleships and aircraft carriers, we would transfer the ammunition to an LCT (landing craft, tank), to be delivered to the larger ship. The holds were open most of the day, and cargo operations were a daily routine.

We never ran out of ammunition. Merchant ships, usually Victory

First Division, USS Pyro *(At right on top row)*

ships, would bring ammunition from the United States, come along-side the *Pyro*, and transfer the ammunition to us.

Across the entrance to the harbor to Espiritu Santo, the Navy had placed a steel mesh net. The purpose of the net was to prevent a Japanese submarine, especially a two-man suicide submarine, from entering the harbor. A small net-tender boat with a small crew was on duty at the entrance at all times. The net would be pulled back to allow the entrance or exit of a United States ship or other friendly ship.

Soon after I came aboard, the Executive Officer gave me several assignments. First of all, I was assigned to the First Division as Assistant Division Officer. The First and Second Divisions were known as the "deck gang." Each division had about fifty men, the majority of them being young men, many of them just out of high school. The First Division was responsible for the maintenance of the forward half of the ship and for handling the cargo operations at the forward three hatches. The Second Division was responsible for the maintenance of the after half of the ship and for handling the cargo operations at the after two hatches.

On learning that I knew how to type, the Executive Officer assigned me to four hours of duty in the coding room each day. Messages from Pearl Harbor and between ships came to the coding room. As a young Ensign it was exciting to know what was happening in the war in the Pacific. We made sure that the Captain was kept informed on all important activities.

In addition to my duties as Assistant Division Officer and in the coding room, I began standing watches on the bridge with the older officers. The bridge is on the topside of the ship's structure with the enclosed wheelhouse in the middle and uncovered portions on each side, known as wings of the bridge. "Standing watch" was the right terminology, as we never sat down.

Over the years the Navy has adopted a watch schedule as follows: evening or first watch, 8:00 PM to 12:00 midnight; midwatch, midnight to 4:00 AM; morning watch, 4:00 AM to 8:00 AM; forenoon watch, 8:00 AM to noon; afternoon watch, noon to 4:00 PM; and then two two-hour watches that were called dog watches, the first dog watch being from 4:00 PM to 6:00 PM and the second dog watch being from 6:00 PM to 8:00 PM. We rotated our watches so that we never had the same watch two days in a row. For about three years of my life, my sleep was constantly interrupted by the watch schedule. The senior officer on the bridge was called the Officer of the Deck (OOD). I was serving as junior officer of the deck (JOOD). At the end of each watch, the OOD enters in the ship's log what happened during his watch.

Each deck division had four or five boatswain's mates who had been in the Navy for several years. We young Ensigns always listened to what they recommended. However, as to one matter we should have used better judgment. We had twelve life rafts, six on each side of the ship. The life rafts were oblong shaped with the rims being cork covered with canvas and with rope netting inside the rim. Each life raft had a keg of water and a tin box containing hardtack.

One day one of the boatswain's mates mentioned that we probably should add more food and water to each raft, and we young officers readily agreed. Then a few days later he suggested that we put a package of orange dye in each raft. He explained that if dye was placed in the water, men in airplanes could spot the life raft more readily. We thought that was a good idea. Then another one of the boatswain's mates recommended that we also add some flares that could be used to attract a plane at night. Again we all agreed. And so it went. We added fishing tackle, oars, a sail, and even cigarettes with waterproof matches to each raft.

One morning after we had our usual morning muster, the Captain suggested that we test one of the life rafts. We walked over to the side of the ship, and one of the boatswain's mates hit the lever that released one of the life rafts. The life raft hit the water with a big splash. The Captain, boatswain's mates, and we division officers looked over the side of the ship. The only thing afloat was the cork rim. The rope netting had torn loose, and everything else had gone straight to the bottom. I had been a boy scout in my younger days, and the scout's motto was "Be Prepared." However, in this case it is obvious that we went too far.

During the rest of the day I was expecting the Captain's yeoman to come to me and say that the Captain wanted to see me, but it never happened. He must have figured that I had suffered enough. Later on we all joked about the overloaded life raft.

The wardroom was the compartment where the officers ate their meals. Due to watches on the bridge and in the engine room, we were never all together at one time. On the *Pyro*, the Captain did not eat in the wardroom, as his meals were served to his cabin. The Executive Officer sat at the head of our table.

The wardroom was a great place. In addition to being the place where an officer ate his meals, it was the place where one could find someone to talk to and enjoy a cup of coffee any time of the day or night. The coffee pot was always on the burner, and an apple was usually available. Most of us would stop by the wardroom before going on watch or getting off watch. Gin rummy was one of our favorite forms of recreation.

I always felt at ease in the wardroom. We referred to each other by nickname. In the wardroom, I was "Cookie," but out on deck I was called "Mr. Cook." The nickname of one of the officers was "Choo Choo." His hometown was Chattanooga, Tennessee, and at that time a popular song was "Chattanooga Choo Choo." In the wardroom he was "Choo Choo," but out on deck he was "Mr. Smith."

On occasion we would listen to short wave radio from Tokyo and Hong Kong, but some of the reports were a little wild. One day it was reported that people were starving to death in Chicago.

Occasionally when cargo operations were heavy and the deck crew was getting worn out, some of us younger officers would jump down into the holds and help out. We soon learned why some of the crew had large biceps.

As often as we could, at anchor we would have a movie in the evening on top of the holds where the ammunition was stored. The movies were the same movies that were being shown in the States and were sent to a base ship in the harbor, usually a repair ship. About every day someone from our ship would go by whaleboat, a small double-ended boat, over to the base ship, return a movie, and pick a new one. The movie officer was a popular man. Everybody except the men on watch would attend the movies. Also, smaller craft in the harbor would send over men to see the movies. On one occasion the reels were out of order and we saw the ending of the movie in the middle of the show. Nobody seemed to mind, but the movie officer had to endure some kidding in the wardroom.

Occasionally we would be given permission to go to shore for a couple of hours. Although we complained about being stuck out in no man's land, Espiritu Santo was a beautiful island with coral beaches. It has been said that James Michener had Espiritu Santo in mind when he wrote his *Tales of the South Pacific*.

With the cruisers and destroyers coming alongside and with working parties from the battleships and aircraft carriers coming aboard, we always kept up to date on the progress of the war in the Pacific. In the early morning of July 13, 1943, the cruiser *USS St. Louis* (CL-49) was engaged in the Battle of Kolombangara near the Solomon Islands. The *St. Louis* took a torpedo, which hit well forward and twisted her bow but caused no serious casualties.[3] Not having an anchor, the cruiser came to Espiritu Santo and tied up alongside the *Pyro* for temporary repairs. She then steamed back to Mare Island in California to complete the repair work.

While at Espiritu Santo we were never subject to a major air attack. However, occasionally a single Japanese plane would fly over the harbor at the high altitude and drop a few bombs. To my knowledge no ship was ever hit nor any damage done. Because of the repetitive sound of the motor we called the Japanese pilot "Sewing Machine Charlie."

During our stay at Espiritu Santo, I had received a radio message through the Red Cross giving me the sad news that my father, Fred Cook, had died on May 21, 1943. I am sure that the Red Cross did the best that it could do under wartime conditions, but I did not receive the message until ten days after his death. I received a lot of support from my fellow officers. Later my mother informed me that she had received a kind letter from "Doc" Norconk, the doctor on the ship.

On August 2, 1943, we received orders to go to Noumea, New Caledonia. New Caledonia was an island about 150 miles long and located south of the New Hebrides Islands. It was French territory, with Noumea being the capital. Located at the southern end of the island, Noumea was one of the United States Navy's principal anchorages in the South Pacific, especially during the first part of World War II.

CHAPTER 3

BACK TO THE STATES

After three days at sea, we anchored in the harbor at Noumea. For the next nine days we carried on cargo operations and transferred ammunition to several ships. Then we received the news that we were going back to the States for an overhaul of the ship and time for leave.

We spent the next twenty-four days at sea, from Noumea to San Francisco. Our average speed was eleven knots, about twelve and a half miles per hour, and with zigzagging—as a protection from Japanese submarines— our forward progress was even less. It was a long, slow trip. From sunset to sunrise we had "darken ship," meaning we blackened out all lights visible from outside the ship. This also meant no cigarettes on deck at night. At sea we wore either a life jacket or a life belt or had one close at hand.

It was during this trip back to the States that I started to stand watches on the bridge with a senior officer while underway. With the senior officers we had on the *Pyro*, I received the best training a young officer could receive.

In one corner of the wheelhouse we had a chart table with a green curtain around it. On the chart table was a chart showing the ship's course and also several patterns to be used in zigzagging. Whenever we were in waters where Japanese submarines might be patrolling, we followed a zigzag course. Zigzag is a series of relatively short, straight-line variations from the base course. The reason for zigzagging was to prevent an enemy submarine from getting an accurate bearing on the ship in order to fire its torpedoes. The light at the chart table was a red light. On a night watch with a darkened ship our eyes would adjust easier to the darkness with the red light rather than with a white light.

Although we usually complained about having a midwatch—from midnight to four in the morning—it actually had some advantages. Except for the men on watch, the crew and officers were in their bunks, and all was quiet and peaceful. Being on the bridge with a full moon was an awesome experience. I felt that I was "sitting on top of the world."

We learned that when another ship is approaching, due to the curvature of the earth, at first all to be seen is the top of the mast. Then as the ship gets closer, the topside of the ship comes into view, and finally the whole ship.

We made one stop on our way to San Francisco, and it was great. We stopped for oil at Bora Bora, one of the Society Islands and located north of Tahiti. It was under French rule, but soon after Pearl Harbor the United States had established a base there. James Michener had said that Bora Bora was the most beautiful island in the world, and I would agree. A blue lagoon with a small mountain covered with green foliage in the background. While oil was being pumped from a tanker to our ship, another Ensign, Bob Blanding, and I were leaning on the rail at the stern of the ship, taking in all the beautiful surroundings. We could see and hear the people on shore—fishing and swimming, laughing and singing. We had a discussion about who was the most civilized—the people on shore or ourselves, who were sitting on an ammunition ship and fighting a war.

The Captain did not allow anybody to go ashore that day. I vowed that someday I would make it back to Bora Bora. It took a long time, but in 1985 my wife, Dolly, and I with two of our daughters spent several days at Bora Bora. When the hotel manager, being French, learned that I had been to Bora Bora during the war, he had a beautiful lei delivered to Dolly.

After a long journey, the *Pyro* finally arrived at San Francisco Bay on September 7, 1943. We docked at Alameda on the east side of the bay. Whenever we were tied up to a dock we put rat guards on the mooring lines. Rat guards are conical metal shields secured around the mooring lines to prevent rats from coming aboard.

During the next two months, the ship was completely overhauled and painted. The 1.1 pom-poms were replaced by four 40-millimeter guns for better anti-aircraft protection.

The best news—we all had a chance to go home for leave. I took a plane home to Mishawaka, Indiana, where my mother was waiting. It was emotional seeing each other, especially since my father had died in the meantime. I spent the week visiting family members, neighbors, and friends. One of the main topics of conversation was gasoline rationing. It was great being able to sleep as late as I wanted to. After a year in the Navy, I finally did not have to get up at a certain time, and my sleep was not interrupted. When it came time to report back to San Francisco, I was ready and eager to go.

Thirty of the crew left as single men and came back as married men. One sailor on the ship had married the same woman for the third time.

Before we departed, we attended various training schools. I was in charge of a group of twenty-one sailors who attended an anti-aircraft training center near San Francisco. To my surprise, the head of the training center was Russell Myers, who prior to the war had been principal at Mishawaka High School, Mishawaka, Indiana. I had graduated from this high school prior to his tenure, but we were personally well acquainted.

While at port the officers and crew had liberty—a chance to go into town for the evening. One night while on watch, I was standing at the gangway as the sailors were returning from liberty. One sailor coming aboard had a torn uniform and a black eye, and his hat was missing. It was obvious he had been in a brawl of some kind. I said to him, "What happened to you?" As he saluted me, he replied, "Sir, never call the Army the Home Guard."

Before going back to sea, we had changes in our assignments. Commander Michael Toal was leaving the ship for another assignment, and Lieutenant Commander T. D. Price was the new Executive Officer. I was now the First Division Officer and also the ship's service officer. Every morning at 8:15, all divisions were mustered on deck. The Division Officer made announcements, gave the day's routine and inspected the men for personal appearance. We had to see that our men were in clean clothes and shaven. It was surprising to see how neat the men looked compared to when they first came aboard.

Every day I inspected the crew's quarters, where the bunks were three deep. Frequently I would find something stuck under a mattress—a book, a magazine, dirty clothes, letters from home. The men always kept the head spotless. Life aboard ship was about as clean a life as one could have.

As Division Officer, I was responsible for advancements in rating, such as from Seaman, second class, to Seaman, first class. The men had to study and pass tests before receiving a higher rating. Although I was only twenty-five years of age some of the younger men in the First Division called me "the old man".

As the ship's Service Officer, I was in charge of the barbershop and the ship's laundry. We had one barber and three men in the laundry. Haircuts were 20 cents for the enlisted men and 25 cents for the officers. Laundry for the crew was a flat rate of 1 dollar a month. An officer paid for his laundry according to the pieces he had laundered that week, but it was never more than 3 dollars a month. The "big bonus" I received for being the ship's Service Officer was free haircuts and laundry.

During the war all letters leaving the ship had to be censored. Since "Doc" Norconk, as Head Censor, did not have time to censor all of the outgoing mail, some of us junior officers assisted him. A letter writer

Officers on the Pyro

was not allowed to mention where we were, where we were going, or what we were doing. If someone did, we cut it out of the letter, leaving an empty square where the forbidden words had been.

Overall, the job was rather amusing. Most of the writers would spend about three pages going nowhere. And I found out that we all agreed on one thing—"The chow is good."

With a full load of ammunition we left the San Francisco Bay area on November 11, 1943, our destination being Brisbane, Australia. It was another long, slow trip. However, we did have a couple of interesting experiences. On the way to Australia we made a stop at Pago Pago in the Samoa Islands. After we had dropped anchor we noticed some native boys swimming close by. There were six or seven of them, all about nine or ten years old and in their "birthday suits." Several of us were standing by the ship's railing, and we motioned for them to come over. We started throwing pennies over the side. As the pennies hit the water and started to drift down, the boys would grab them and stick them in their mouths. Soon their cheeks were puffed with pennies. We were laughing, and the boys were having a great time. For a while the war seemed far away.

Boatswain's Mates, First Division, on the Pyro *—*
Knopski, Edwards, Moore, Beyer and Evans

A couple of days later, we witnessed two waterspouts—about the craziest thing I have ever seen. A waterspout is a whirling column of air and water extending from a cloud to the surface of the ocean—like a tornado on the sea. Fortunately, we observed them at a distance.

About every day we had some kind of a drill—fire, collision, abandon ship, General Quarters, and gun drills. During a General Quarters drill, when every man was at his battle station, the Captain would try to make the drill as realistic as possible by reporting bombs and torpedoes striking at certain locations. At one drill the Captain sent out the word that a bomb had struck the fantail, exploding in the second deck. A few minutes later the Captain asked what was being done back there. The young officer in charge, not knowing what to do, reported that nothing could be done, as all of his men had been killed. However, on Captain's orders, he soon had them resurrected and fighting the fire.

Dr. A. A. Norconk and crew with a catch in the South Pacific

CHAPTER 4

THE BIG DANCE

After twenty-five days at sea, we finally arrived at our destination, Brisbane, Australia. As our new assignment we were to become part of the Seventh Fleet, and our immediate job was to transport ammunition from Australia to New Guinea. The Seventh Fleet was known as "MacArthur's Navy." General Douglas MacArthur had his headquarters in Brisbane and was in command of what was known as the Southwest Pacific Area. Our ship news bulletins always began with the following phrase: "MacArthur says." During the next seven months we made four trips to New Guinea, three from Brisbane and one from Sydney. Our most frequent port in New Guinea was Milne Bay on the southern tip of the island. As the war progressed, we anchored at other locations on the north side of New Guinea —Buna, Finschhaven, and finally Hollandia.

Viewing the island from the ship, New Guinea was a beautiful sight. When we went ashore we found it to be hot and muggy. Once when the ship was anchored at Milne Bay, another officer and I went ashore for a couple of hours. Rather than hike into the jungle, we decided to take off our shoes and wade up a small creek into the jungle. After several minutes of wading, we heard a rustling sound at one side of the creek. We were a bit frightened at first, but soon we saw a native man. With a big smile on his face, he said, "Hi." He had bushy hair and was wearing a loincloth. Around his neck was a cord, and attached to the cord was a pack of Lucky Strike cigarettes. We cheerfully said "hi" back to him. It was obvious that he had been in contact with some American soldiers.

Part of our trip going to and coming back from New Guinea was inside the Great Barrier Reef. We always enjoyed that part of the trip. Not only was the scenery beautiful, but it was also an area in which it was difficult for submarines to operate. However, one night we had a rough time. We got caught in a bad storm with strong winds, so we dropped anchor. Anchors are made to dig into the mud, but inside the Great Barrier Reef, the bottom is hard coral. Our anchor was dragging on the bottom, and the storm was pushing the ship toward a reef. We kept our boilers fired, and we steamed into the wind. Fortunately, we were able to hold our position until the storm subsided, and then we continued our trip.

On our return to Brisbane on February 13, 1944, after our second trip to New Guinea a new Captain came aboard. Captain Boller had received a new assignment and was returning to the States. After a brief ceremony, Commander A. B. Dickie became our new skipper. We soon discovered that his policy was "work hard, then play hard." On the second day after he came aboard, he called me to his cabin and asked me how much money we had in the Ship Service account. I told him that we had around 3,000 dollars. "Wow," he said, "Let's have a dance." He authorized Ensign Bob Blanding, the Second Division Officer, and me to arrange for two dances on two different nights, half of the crew on one night and the other half of the crew on the second night.

On the *Pyro* we carried a station wagon. When we hit a port such as Brisbane we had mobility. Bob and I, with other officers, went right to work and lined up the best dance hall we could find, the Cantwell Studios at 463 Adelaide Street, and also the best dance orchestra we could find. The first dance (for the port watch) was scheduled for Wednesday night, March 1st, and the second dance (for the starboard watch) was scheduled for Monday night, March 6th. At muster one morning we told the crew that either we could arrange through the Red Cross and other agencies for girls to come to the dance, or they could invite the girls on their own. The vote was almost unanimous that they could handle that problem without any outside help. We told them that any girl who came to the door would have to tell us who had invited her.

The Australian boys had been fighting in north Africa and Europe for two years before the United States even entered the war. A dance with American sailors was a big deal to the Australian girls in the area.

The night of the first dance arrived, and Bob Blanding and I were standing at the entrance. A group of girls were waiting to come in. As they entered we asked them who had invited them. The first six or seven girls gave the same name. I leaned over to Bob and said, "Oh boy, boo-boo No. 1. We didn't put any limit on how many girls the crew could invite." Well, it all worked out all right since many of the younger sailors had not invited anybody.

The orchestra began to play, and the dance began. It was a great night. Several officers were there with Navy nurses or girls from the Red Cross. The music was the hit songs at the time—"Moonlight Serenade," "Tuxedo Junction," "Chattanooga Choo-Choo," and "Stardust." It was good for the sailors to see the officers in a different light—singing, laughing, dancing.

Many of the sailors on the *Pyro* were musicians. As the dance went along, a sailor from the *Pyro* would ask an Aussie member of the band if he could take over for a while. One would take over on the piano, another on the drums, and another on the trumpet. At one point members of the crew had taken over the entire band. Everybody had a great time, and for one night we forgot about the war.

When we returned to the ship, we learned that we had orders to take off for New Guinea in a couple of days. The dance for the other half of the crew was cancelled. Such was life in wartime.

We learned from the dance that we had enough musicians on board to form a ship's band. In fact, one of the men, before joining the Navy, had played trumpet for a big name band. Hence, we formed a ship's band, and they practiced when they could. Then, often on nights when at anchor and when we had a movie, the ship's band would play several tunes before the movie. The crew loved it. The band became known as the "Pyro-Maniacs."

On our trips to and from New Guinea, we maintained darken ship. All the fighting ships and auxiliary ships followed the same practice with one exception. Twice on our way to New Guinea we passed a ship going in the opposite direction with all the lights on. In both cases it was a United States hospital ship. Even war has some rules—you are not allowed to bomb or torpedo a hospital ship. Hospital ships were unarmed and marked in accordance with the Geneva Convention.

With our continual moving around, it was difficult for the mail service to keep track of us. One day at Milne Bay we received sixteen large bags of mail. I doubt that much work was done during the next two hours. It was always a big day when the mail did arrive.

Sometimes before going on watch I would stop by the wardroom for a cup of coffee. Often I would have conversation with one of the officers who had been on the ship several months before I came aboard. Invariably, with a frown on his face he would proceed to tell me that he could not wait until the day he received orders to leave the *Pyro*. Finally, one day I heard he had received orders for new assignment to another ship. I went to the wardroom. There he was with his cup of coffee and the same frown on his face. I said to him, "Hey, why the sad look? For over a year you have been telling me that the day you got off this tub would be the happiest day of your life." "Yeah, Cookie," he said. "I know that I said that, but to tell the truth, I'd rather stay here and grumble."

Our charts for New Guinea were not too accurate. When we went into Hollandia on June 6, 1944, the Captain ordered a coxswain and me to go ahead of the ship in a whaleboat and take soundings to make sure that the ship could proceed without the danger of going aground on way to the anchorage. I would drop a lead on a line to check the depth of the water. The ship's draft was the depth of the ship beneath the waterline. If the depth of the water was more than the ship's draft, we would motion to the officers on the bridge of the ship to come ahead. Then after going ahead for a short distance, I would take another sounding. We proceeded doing this until we reached our anchorage.

Soon after we had dropped anchor at Hollandia, "Doc" Norconk received orders to return to the States for a new assignment. He was a cheerful man, and often he would be humming or singing a song popular at that time—"When My Baby Smiles at Me." On the day he left the ship, we arranged for the "Pyro-Maniacs," the ship's band, to be at the gangway. As "Doc" went down the accommodation ladder to the boat, the band played his favorite tune, and we all waved goodbye.

On April 17, 1944, I received my silver bars, and I was now a Lieutenant (junior grade), known as Lt. (j.g.). Several of the officers on the *Pyro* had already received orders to return to the States for new assignment. Hence, it was no surprise to me when on June 22, 1944, I received my orders to return to the States and report for duty to APA Pre-Commissioning School, Naval Station, Seattle, Washington. APA is the designation for an attack transport ship. I left the *Pyro* while she was still at anchor at Hollandia.

Although I looked forward to my new assignment, leaving the *Pyro* was not easy. I had spent hundreds of hours on the bridge standing watch with these men. We had played cards together and joked in the wardroom. I kept in contact with several of the officers and crew for many years after the war. In fact, one of the officers, Bob Blanding, and I became the best of friends, and we corresponded until his death in 1992.

I returned to the United States on the *USS Bloemfontein*, a former Dutch ship. I learned that the name is a Dutch word that means "fountain of flowers." While on the *Bloemfontein*, each passenger received a daily mimeographed newsletter called "The Ocean Post." In the July 19, 1944 issue, it was reported that two ammunition ships had blown up at Port Chicago, California. The 10,000-ton *Quinault Victory* and the 7,000-ton *A. E. Bryant* had been loading ammunition at the Naval ammunition supply depot. Port Chicago is located on an arm of the San Francisco Bay, about thirty-five miles northeast of San Francisco. According to the newsletter, the explosion was the worst disaster of its kind in the nation's history, with a death toll of 350. An anchor for one of the ships was found a mile away.

After reading the article, I told my roommates on the *Bloemfontein* that my days on an ammo ship were over, as I was on my way to duty on an attack transport. Little did I know what lay ahead for me.

After arriving in San Francisco, I was given leave to go home for a couple of weeks before reporting to Seattle. Wearing my uniform with my overseas ribbons, I found that I was greeted warmly wherever I went. The United States really seemed to be united in our efforts to win World War II. It did not seem to be a question of who was going to win the war; the only question was when.

THE OCEAN POST   1

Wednesday July 19th 1944

SHAEF - The Allies burst dramatically out of both ends of the Normandie beachhead Tuesday as the Americans on the West conquered the Nazi hinge town of St Lo after a stubborn eight day battle and strong British and Canadian armored forces on the East crossed the Orne river and poured into the Caen plain in a major breakthrough on a full offensive scale Tuesday night as the seventh week of the invasion got under way Nazi marshal Rommel's invasion line was cracked wide open on the side toward Paris, onehundred and twenty miles to the East, was dented in the center and was crumbling on the west flank.

ROME -Allied troops crashed through strongly held German positions Tuesday and swept three miles across open country into the town of Pontedei on the Arno river between Pisa and Florence, reaching the enemy's Gothi defense line and virtually outflanking the great West coast port of Li vorno.

LONDON - Red armies of the South in powerful new offensives have cracked open German defenses around the great bastion of Lwow in old Poland, spilling through reeling Nazi forces for three day gains of thirtyone miles on a 125 mile front, premier marshal Stalin announced Tuesday night Stalin in a broadcast order of theday announced the capture of more than six hundred towns and villages including a network of strategic rail junctions around Lwow.

LONDON - In the greatest display of aerial might since d day Allied air forces hurled more than fffteenhundred heavy bombers and hundreds of lighter planes Thursday into support of gen Sir Bernard Montgomery's new Orne river breakthrough. They delivered seven thousand tons of bombs on German positions in a seventyfive square mile area. A thousand planes from Britain earlier bombed German rocket bomb experimental stations at Peenemunde and Zinnopitz while an Italian based force struck into South west Germany at Friedrichshafen and Memmingen.

LONDON - Hugh Dalton, economic warfare minister informed commons Tuesday that Britain was trying to obtain an agreement with the United States to regulate the industrial switch from wartime to peacetime production questionsx and answers disclosed disturbed feelings about markets in view of the efforts of US war production shief Donald Nelson to permit American industry to return partly to production of civilian goods.

PORT CHICAGO CALIF - An explosion of two naval ammunition ships in the worst disaster of its kind in the nation's history left a toll of 350 deaths today as rescue workers poked through rubble in search of more bodies. The twin blasts late last night, shaking 14 counties and felt 80 miles away shattered this town of 1500 and wrecked two freighters, the ten thousand ton Quinault Victory and the seven thousand ton E A Bryant, loading ammunition at the port Chicago naval ammunition supply depot. The blasts sprayed hot metal at the port Chicago area over a section of two miles. One ships abchor was found a mile away. The port Chicago depot is in an arm of the San Francisco bay, some 35 miles Nort east of San Francisco. Most of the dead were negro members of navy loading crews at the port of Chicago ammunition magzzine. In addition poc sibly 70 members of the crews of the two ships lost their lives..A num ber of civilian workers on the docks were killed. The list of injured may reach one thousand, including those cut by flying glass. Nearly every window in port Chicago was broken. One man a mile away said he saw a mile high skyrocket of red and white flames leap into the clouds Two small coast guard boats were sunk by the explosions. Wreckage swept over Suisun bay which branches East from San Francisco bay. Describing the explosion of the two ammunition ships captain Gois said: "We have no reason for giving any cause for the explosion as there were no close survivors to give evidence of what happened."Captain Gois said nine officers were missing and considered killed. The rest of the enlisted men not of the ships crew missing were twohundred. Damage to the mercha ships runs into millions of dollars. Sheriff James M Long said that casualties had occurred within the badly damahed town of port of Chicago itself.

A copy of the newsletter "The Ocean Post" that was distributed on the Bloemfontein

GEN EISENHOWERS ADVANCED COMMAND POST - On the night that Brig Gen
Theodore Roosevelt died in Normandy Gen Eisenhower was preparing an
order promoting him to major general in command of a division. Secretary
Stimson disclosed this tuesday and added that on his trip to Normandy
"I was privileged to see the grave of my old friend whose death was a
very sad thing to me."

NEW YORK - The Berlin radio which frequently broadcasts reports in
attempts to glean information said tuesday that President Roosevelt
soon would visit Rome and that arrangements already had been made for
his trip by his Vatican representative Myron C Taylor. There was nothing from any other source to indicate that the German report had any
basis of truth.

LONDON - The London daily Mirror boosted Gen Sir Bernard Montgomery as
a possible candidate for parliament after the war in its lead editorial
tuesday entitled "Monty Mr."

WASHINGTON - Arrival of a Brazilian expeditionary force in Naples July
sixteenth to foin allied armies in operation on the Italian front was
announced tuesday by the war department. Brazils action in sending
troops abroad marked the first time that any troops from Latin America
have participated in an European war.

LONDON - A British army spokesman in a BBC broadcast directed to the
German armed forces warned tuesday that punishment would be meted out
without mercy to any German soldier known to have committed an atrocity.
This warning came sunday after the German radio had rejected Gen Eisenhowers demand that french forces of the interior be treated as regular
soldiers under his command.

BERN - Admiral Nicholas Horthy of Hungary has promised the international
red cross committee that no more Jews will be transported forcibly out
of Hungary it was learned tuesday and authorized the committee to direct
evacuation of Jewish children to countries willing to receive them.

WASHINGTON - Secretary of state Hull indicated tuesday that the forth-
coming talks on world peace organization here next month would be held
at the expert level rather than by the foreign ministers of Russia the
United States Britain and China.

NEW YORK - The condition of Miss Catherine Searless of Rahway NJ whose
right arm was chewed off at the elbow by a nine hundred pound Polar
bear was reported as good tuesday at Roosevelt hospital where the twenty
four year old girl monday underwent an amputation of the remainder of
the limb. A male bear in Central Park Zoo gnawed Miss Searless arm early
monday police reported after she had climbed over an iron guard rail
and waved a handkerchief at the sleeping animal.

CHICAGO - Ambitions to become a state that have cherished by the people
of Hawaii for more than forty years are being given new expression in
activities of the Hawaii delegation to the democratic national convention. The delegation is backing a declaration on the statehood which it
hopes to get into the party platform.

CHICAGO - A sharp drive by the CIO to renominate Henry Wallace and t
head off the candidacy of the war mobilization director James F Byrnes
tuesday spotlighted Senator Harry Truman of Missouri as a possible cam-
proming for the democratic vice presidential nomination. CIO president
Philip Murray who forced a poll of the Pensylvania delegation which dis
closed fortyone of its seventytwo votes were for Wallace republican
news informed convention leaders that the labor organization would not
stand for Byrnes nomination. There were indications that Wallaces dele-
gate strength was slipping away despite the CIO efforts and apparently
authentic reports spread that Truman might be the labor leaders second
choice if Wallace cannot make the grade.

After my leave in Indiana, I took a train to Seattle. The train was crowded with soldiers and sailors. When the train stopped at a town in North Dakota, several women came aboard and passed out pheasant sandwiches wrapped in wax paper to every man in uniform. It is my understanding that some women from this town were doing this every day until the end of the war.

U.S.S. PYRO

Friday, 12 May, 1944.

At anchor.

PLAN OF THE DAY

Port routine except as follows:

0000	1st, 2nd, and 8th working parties relieve.
0630	Early breakfast for 3rd and 4th working parties.
0700	3rd and 4th working parties relieve.
0815	Muster on stations.
0830	MWB trip to shore with Paymaster – return immediately.
1200	Dinner for 5th and 6th working parties.
1230	5th and 6th working parties relieve.
1245	MWB trip to shore with mail orderly – return immediately.
1730	Supper for 1st and 2nd working parties.
1800	1st and 2nd working parties relieve.
2330	Lunch for 3rd and 4th working parties.
2440	3rd and 4th working parties relieve.
NOTES:	Continue working cargo 'round the clock, as directed by cargo officers.

T.D. PRICE,
Lt-Cdr., USNR
Executive Officer.

Typical Plan of the Day (at New Guinea)

During the war all the hotels and restaurants were crowded. While in Seattle another officer and I went to a dining room in a hotel for dinner. About a dozen people were waiting in line for a table. We were in uniform with our overseas ribbons. Without exception, all of the people in the line motioned for us to go to the front of the line, saying, "Hey, you boys go first."

I spent about three months in Seattle attending the APA Pre-Commissioning School, most of the time going to navigation classes. I moved to Astoria, Oregon, and stayed at a B.O.Q. (Bachelor Officer Quarters). Here again I was attending classes in navigation.

CHAPTER 5

ANOTHER AMMO SHIP

It was Saturday night, November 25, 1944, in Astoria, Oregon. Looking forward to a quiet weekend, I had picked up a local newspaper and retired to my room at the B.O.Q. While stretched out on the bed reading the newspaper, I received a telephone call from the Navy at Seattle. I was informed that I had orders to report aboard a ship that night at Astoria. A sailor with the orders was leaving Seattle by automobile and would arrive at Astoria around 2:30 AM, and this is exactly what happened. Rather than calling my mother in the middle of the night and upsetting her, I wrote a quick note giving her my new address. I did not get a chance to say goodbye to my friends at the B.O.Q. I even left behind at the local laundry a bag full of dirty laundry that I had dropped off the day before—socks, shirts, and underwear.

In the car that picked me up was an officer who had received his orders that night and had come down from Seattle. The officer was John H. Moss. We both had orders to report for duty on the *USS Las Vegas Victory* (AK-229), he as the First Lieutenant and I as the Navigator. The First Lieutenant is in charge of the equipment and ship maintenance. The Navigator plots the ship's course, checks on the ship's location, makes sure that the ship reaches its destination on schedule, and keeps the ship's log.

Fortunately, I had received top-notch training in navigation by Commander Michael Toal, the Executive Officer on the *Pyro*. In addition, I had been going to navigation schools for the past several weeks. Hence, I felt prepared for taking on the duties as Navigator on the *Las Vegas Victory*. Being on the bridge of the ship and navigating with the stars seemed to be the right spot for me. Although the new assignment came up fast, I was excited and ready to go.

The sailor driving the car took us down to the Columbia River to the dock where a Coast Guard boat was waiting for us. Rain was pouring down as we threw our gear into the boat. The boat shoved off, and the two of us went below, where the coxswain gave each of us a cup of hot coffee. I turned to Lt. Moss and asked what this was all about. He said that it appeared that the *Las Vegas Victory* needed a First Lieutenant and a Navigator before it left the States. I told him that I had never been a Navigator, and he said that he had never been a First Lieutenant and that this would be his first time at sea. We both started laughing, and the coxswain joined in.

The ship was anchored about eight miles upstream. After a bumpy, wet ride we pulled up alongside the ship. A rope ladder was dropped over the side, and the two of us climbed aboard with our gear. I had received my orders around 2:30 AM, and I was aboard the ship around 4:00 AM. That had to be some kind of record. The Executive Officer, Lt. Manuel Vigil, welcomed us aboard and took me to my cabin, which was located below the chartroom. On the way to my quarters, he gave me two items of information. First, the ship had a supply of food for a whole year. And second, it was an ammunition ship. After I had dropped off my gear, I went directly to the chartroom, as the ship was getting underway at 6:00 AM.

USS Las Vegas Victory *(AK229)*

The second statement by Lt. Vigil hit me as a surprise. AK229 in large letters and numerals was painted on the bow of the ship. The AK designation on a ship would indicate that it was a cargo ship. AE was the designation for ammunition ships. My first ship, the *USS Pyro*, had painted on its bow in large letters and numerals AE1. Well, anyway, for me it was from one ammo ship to another.

The *USS Las Vegas Victory* had been built for the Maritime Commission by the Permante Metals Corporation in Richmond, California. She was one of the ten Victory ships taken over by the Navy to transport ammunition to the forward areas of the Pacific. Hard to believe, but each of these Victory ships had been built in 45 days or less.[4] She had been named by the Maritime Commission in honor of the city of Las Vegas, Nevada, and the Navy retained the name. Incidentally, at that time the population of the city of Las Vegas was less than 25,000.

I did not know it at the time, but I learned later that the drive shaft that drove the ship through the water and also the large bearings around the drive shaft in the Victory ships were manufactured in my hometown, Mishawaka, Indiana, at the Dodge Manufacturing Company. The 19-inch diameter drive shaft was supported by a bearing every twenty feet between the steam engine and the propeller of the ship. In 1944 the company received the Army/Navy "E" for Excellence award. The huge pennant flew proudly over the plant in Mishawaka. A star was added to it in 1945, signifying that Dodge had kept up its high standards through the end of the war.[5]

The *Las Vegas Victory* had a tonnage of 15,100, a length of 455 feet, and a beam (width) of 62 feet. The ship's draft was 29 feet, 2 inches. This was a fact that we had to remember when we traveled into shallow waters.

The ship had neither radar nor loran. Loran was relatively new at that time and was a device for determining a ship's position by means of pulsed signals sent out by two known radio stations.

Our armament consisted of one 5-inch gun on the stern, one 3-inch gun on the bow, and four 20-millimeter guns on each side. Our top speed was 15.5 knots or approximately 17.8 miles per hour.

Before its stop at Astoria, the *Las Vegas Victory* had docked up the Columbia river at Beaver, Oregon, where the Seabees had loaded the ship with 7,600 tons of ammo.

The *Las Vegas Victory* in its five holds carried ammunition for United States Navy ships—battleships, cruisers, destroyers, and aircraft carriers. Included in our cargo were the following: projectiles, powder, and cartridges for 16-inch, 6-inch, 5-inch, and 3-inch caliber guns; smoke pots; and bombs of all sizes—2,000 pounds, 1,000 pounds, 500 pounds, 250 pounds, and 100 pounds.

Looking down into one of the holds and seeing all that ammo made one realize that duty on an ammunition ship was different from duty on any other type of ship. One bomb, one torpedo, or a fire, and it could be "curtains." To keep life on the bright side we would tell a new sailor when he came aboard that one of the advantages of serving on an ammunition ship was that we never had to worry about running out of ammo.

The Captain of the *Las Vegas Victory* was Lieutenant Commander William F. Lally, who prior to the war had been a lawyer in New York City. He had served in the Navy during World War I. The Gunnery Officer was Lieutenant (j.g.) Harry Scherer, Jr., a young lawyer from West Virginia. And I—a lawyer yet to be—was the Navigator, the officer responsible for the safe navigation of the ship. I am sure that many persons would think that a ship with lawyers as the Skipper, the Gunnery Officer, and the Navigator was headed for the shoals.

Officers on the Las Vegas Victory

The engineering officer was Lieutenant Levin B. Hannigan, who had been an instructor at a boys' academy. Three of the officers had been in the business world before the war: Lieutenant John H. Moss, the first lieutenant; Lieutenant Kirby B. Payne, communication officer; and Ensign Richard G. Maloney, assistant communication officer.

Three of the officers were recent college graduates: Ensign Edward C. Christoph, signal officer; Ensign Michael H. Jordan, Jr., first division officer; and Ensign Melvin H. Day, second division officer. All of these officers had been in civilian life prior to World War II. Wisely, the Navy mixed in with us ex-civilians several officers who had been in the Navy for several years. The executive officer, Lieutenant Manuel Virgil, and the assistant engineering officer, Lieutenant (j.g.) Andrew Kukuvka, were two of them. Both of them had been enlisted men who were made officers during the war. Such officers were known as "mustangs." We relied on these men.

We also had three warrant officers: Lewis A. Frick, boatswain; Jess Mangus, gunner; and John P. Koldin, machinist. Warrant officers also had been enlisted men. They were senior to all chief petty officers and junior to all commissioned officers. Altogether we had fifteen officers. We had a good mix of backgrounds and experience aboard, and we got along great.

We did not have a doctor, dentist, or chaplain. However, when we were at anchor one could go to a nearby ship if the services of one of these professional men were needed.

The *Las Vegas Victory* had a small crew of 100 men. Many of them were just out of high school or had left high school to join the Navy. For most of them it was their first time at sea. We had no barber, but often one of the cooks would do the job or, at least try to do the job, usually while one sat on a bitt, a short steel post on the ship's stern.

The citizens of Las Vegas were honored to have a ship bear the name of their city and sent to the ship books and magazines for a ship library.

My cabin was really nice. In addition to a bunk bed, I had a washbasin, a desk, a storage bin that could be used as a seat, a closet, and a porthole with fan.

CHAPTER 6

THREE STORMY DAYS

Although I had not had any sleep the night before, I was in the chartroom at 6:00 AM, making preparations to take off. The chartroom was directly behind the wheelhouse, and all of the equipment was new. After introducing myself to the quartermaster and the signalmen, I started to lay out the ship's course.

Like Magellan, we were still navigating by the stars in those days. On an ordinary day at sea, the navigator's routine would be as follows: First, just before sunrise he takes sights by his sextant on two or three stars and plots the ship's position from those readings. Then, during the day the navigator takes two or three sights of the sun to verify the ship's position. Right after sunset he takes sights on the stars again. To me it was absolutely amazing that you could take sights on the stars, millions of miles away, to determine your position at sea down to a tenth of a mile.

The navigator has to lay down courses and figure out times for change of course. He has to take into consideration tides, winds, and currents. When in sight of land he has to take bearings on peaks and objects on shore to fix the ship's position. He must study the charts carefully to make sure that the ship keeps clear of any reefs or rocks. Fortunately, for the first several days we would be sailing in a westerly direction into the blue Pacific with no rocks, shoals, or islands ahead.

My first three days as a navigator were rough—no stars, no sun, and rough seas. Three stormy days in a row with clouds and heavy rain. It was rugged.

Without the stars for sights and without any land to take bearings on, the navigator has to determine the ship's position by what is known as "dead reckoning." He plots the ship's course and, taking into consideration the ship's speed, the wind and ocean currents, tries to determine the ship's position. With wind and rough seas, the ship's speed varied. Often due to heavy winds and strong currents, the position determined by "dead reckoning" could be miles from the actual location.

Due to the rough seas, the ship pitched and rolled. Being their first time at sea, many of the crew were seasick, and some of them never got out of their "sacks."

Added to our woes were problems with our cargo. In the No. 4 hold, the shoring that held the 1,000-pound bombs in place had broken loose, and the bombs were rolling back and forth, making a racket that could be heard topside. To our relief, the Executive Officer, the Gunner, and the Boatswain went below and, with help from some of the crew, were able to get the bombs propped up safely.

On the afternoon of the second day at sea, the Captain conferred with me in the chartroom. He was concerned and rightly so. Not only was this his first command, but it was my first time as Navigator. Furthermore, we were off to a rough start. The two of us went out to the starboard wing of the bridge. The ship was pitching, the wind was howling, and we were getting drenched. We decided to go amidship. We moved to the open deck in front of the wheelhouse. Suddenly, both of our faces were splattered with something other than water. We wiped our faces and discovered that we had been hit by vomit. A young sailor was on lookout duty in the crow's nest on the forward mast. Apparently the pitching and rolling of the ship was a little more than he could take. The captain and I decided that it was time to go into the wheelhouse. Not right then but at later times, we were able to laugh about the incident.

After three days of stormy weather, the clouds disappeared and the sea became calm. The Pacific had finally become pacific. For the first time since leaving Astoria I was able to take sights of the stars and sun. On our eighth day at sea, we had our first landfall—our first sighting of land—on Molokai, one of the Hawaiian Islands. Later we passed by Diamond Head on the island of Oahu. Although we did not stop, the young sailors stood along the railing, waving their hands and cheering upon seeing land.

Our first stop would be at Eniwetok, a large, isolated atoll in the northwestern corner of the Marshall Islands. An atoll is a circular ring of low, sandy islets and an ideal spot for a ship to anchor.

In the chartroom we had a fathometer, an instrument to measure the depth of the water. It worked by sending a sound down through the water to be echoed back from the bottom of the sea. As we were approaching Eniwetok, I was alone in the chartroom and watching the fathometer. I noticed that the depth of the water below the ship started to decrease rapidly. A ship cannot be stopped like an automobile. You have no brakes, and even when you stop the engines, the ship continues to drift forward. The depth as shown on the fathometer continued to drop, and I feared the worse—a reef up ahead.

I had noticed in studying my charts that reefs in the Pacific had been named for the ship that was shipwrecked on that reef. One thing was for sure—I did not want a reef to be named the Las Vegas Reef. Just as I was about to charge into the wheelhouse and shout "Stop all engines!" the fathometer showed that the depth was beginning to level off. This young navigator could not have been any happier.

As we entered Eniwetok I noticed on our port side a brand new tanker stranded on a reef. As we passed by I thought to myself, "That poor, unlucky guy—the Navigator."

Taking a sight as Navigator on the
Las Vegas Victory

We dropped anchor and stayed overnight at Eniwetok. We had been at sea for two weeks. The Navy had considered it safe to travel from Astoria to Eniwetok without escort for protection. Our stop at Eniwetok was for the purpose of joining other ships and having escort the rest of the way. The next stop would be Ulithi, part of the Caroline Islands. This time we were in convoy with another ammunition ship and two oilers, with two destroyer escorts (DEs) for protection.

CHAPTER 7

BABELTHAUP AND GUADACANAL

After four days at sea we arrived safely at Ulithi, where we were at anchor for the next two weeks. Ulithi is a large atoll and was a great anchorage for many ships. Being only ten degrees above the equator, Ulithi was a hot spot. At times the sun would be almost directly overhead. To cool off the hot decks, we placed hoses with running water.

The Navy had designated one of the small islets as a recreational area. The name of the islet was Mog Mog, a name we never forgot. There was nothing on Mog Mog except a few coconut trees. Liberty parties would be taken to Mog Mog by boat for a couple of hours ashore. It was always a good feeling to be off the ship and on land, if only for a short time. When at Mog Mog, some of us would go for a swim.

We spent Christmas Day at Ulithi, and all of us, officers and crew, had turkey and ice cream for dinner. After dinner the officers, including the Captain, gathered in the wardroom, with arms around each other, to sing some Christmas carols. We started each song with much gusto, but, not remembering all the words, we faltered towards the end.

While at Ulithi we unloaded part of our cargo and received additional ammunition from a merchant cargo ship and ammunition lighters. Then on December 30th we left Ulithi on our way to Kossol Passage in the Palau Islands, being the western part of the Caro-

39

line Islands, in company with a cargo ship and a destroyer escort. It was a one-day trip, and we anchored within sight of Babelthaup, the most northern and largest of the Palau Islands. In November 1944, the United States Marines had captured the island of Peleliu in the southern part of the Palau Islands. However, it was reported to us that on Babelthaup there were from eighteen to twenty-five thousand Japanese troops and many thousand Japanese civilians. The United States Navy had nothing on shore but several ships at anchor.

January 12, 1945 was a day that we will not forget. Around 8:00 AM the *USS Argonne* (AG-31) reported by flag hoist that an emergency existed: submarine in vicinity. We went to General Quarters and made preparations to get underway. To sound General Quarters is to give the general alarm that will bring all hands to their battle station as quickly as they can get there. By various reports over the TBS (Talk Between Ships), we learned that three Japanese midget submarines had sneaked into the anchorage. From further reports we learned that one of the submarines had surfaced and that one of our ships had fired and sank it. It was later reported that one of the submarines had run into a reef and exploded. We never did find out what happened to the third submarine. In any event, the day ended with no damage to United States ships and no U.S. casualties.

While at Kossol Passage, several ships and boats had come alongside to receive ammunition. On January 24th we headed back to Ulithi, this time in convoy with three merchant ships and two patrol crafts.

After a week of cargo operations at Ulithi, we were sent on a special mission to the island of Guadalcanal to pick up a Marine Parachute unit, along with its observation planes. We were substituting for another ship that had been damaged in a collision.

We had a destroyer escort as protection from Ulithi to Seeadler Harbor, Manus Island, part of the Admiralty Islands. We arrived at Manus on February 1, 1945, and soon heard the tragic story about the *Mount Hood*. On November 10, 1944, the *USS Mount Hood* (AE-11), an ammunition ship, had blown up with 4,500 tons of ammunition at Manus. All of the 350 officers and men on board had been killed instantly. The flying fragments from *Mount Hood* smashed into some 30 other ships and harbor craft, bringing the total casualties to nearly 1,000 killed and wounded.[6]

Many years after the *Mount Hood* disaster I was informed by former shipmates from the *Pyro* two items of information which I did not know at that time. First, the Captain of the *Mount Hood* was Commander Michael Toal, who had been the Executive Officer of the *Pyro* when I first went aboard. He was the officer who really taught me about navigation at sea. He had been my mentor. Also, I was told that the *Pyro* was in Seeadler Harbor at the time of the explosion. Fortunately, the *Pyro* was at a repair dock at a safe distance from the disaster.

On February 3 we continued our trip to Guadalcanal without escort. First we anchored at Tulagi Harbor, Florida Island, and then later at Lunga Point, Guadalcanal, all part of the Solomon Islands. With the Marine planes and equipment aboard, along with two Marine officers, we weighed anchor for our return to Ulithi.

Our first night underway, February 11, 1945, after a busy day I "hit the sack," looking forward to a night of rest. It was a beautiful moonlit night. I had no sooner fallen asleep when I jumped out of my bunk. The bells were clanging, indicating General Quarters. I scrambled up the ladder to the bridge, my station at the time of General Quarters. The Officer of the Deck reported an unidentified object off the starboard bow. Some of the men on the bridge were identifying the object as a Japanese carrier. I went to the starboard wing of the bridge, took out my binoculars, and focused on the carrier. Then I went to the chartroom and studied the chart. I relieved everybody's mind by identifying the "unidentified object" as an island—Buraku Island, twenty miles distant. We all laughed and secured from General Quarters, and I crawled back into my bunk.

We stopped at Manus Island again and picked up a destroyer escort for protection on the remainder of the trip to Ulithi. We arrived at Ulithi on February 17 and stayed there until March 25. During this time we received ammunition from merchant ships that had come from the States, and we discharged ammunition to destroyers and landing crafts and also boats that took the ammunition to larger ships. It was a hot and boring month.

The Navy and the Postal Service did the best they could to get the mail to us, but the way we were moving around it was difficult. People in the States had been advised that if they wanted to mail Christmas gifts and cards to men in service to do so several weeks ahead of time. Hence, my mother and other relatives mailed cookies, gifts, and cards to me in November. However, due to our moving around, I received my Christmas mail on my birthday, March 2nd.

CHAPTER 8

KAMIKAZES

We left Ulithi on March 25 with a large group of ships, but eventually we had a task group consisting of only four ships: our ship; an oiler, *USS Tomahawk* (AO-88); a destroyer, *USS Stockton* (DD-646); and another destroyer, *USS Gillespie* (DD-609). Our destination was Okinawa, and the date for the invasion was April 1, Easter Sunday. However, our date of arrival was set for the day before. The code name for the invasion of Okinawa was "Operation Iceberg." We were to steam in a northwesterly direction until we arrived at a certain point designated on the chart as "Bedbug." On arriving at "Bedbug," we were to head in a westerly direction to Okinawa.

Around 11:30 P.M. we arrived at the turning point. We received a message by TBS from the *USS Stockton* that it had a surface contact about four miles away. Immediately we made a sharp turn to port to course 270 degrees, being straight west. We also increased our speed. A few minutes later the *Stockton* reported to us that the surface contact had changed to a sound contact. This indicated that the contact was a submarine which had dived below the surface. We immediately went to General Quarters and changed our course to 290 degrees.

The *Stockton* was given permission to stay behind and started to drop depth charges. The other three of us, being our ship, the *Tomahawk*, and the *Gillespie* kept on our westerly course. We were anxious to get out of there, and we just zigged and zagged without following any of the zigzag patterns which had been worked out.

We proceeded westerly, and around 8:00 AM on March 31, being "L Day – 1," we arrived at our destination. We anchored at Kerama Retto, a small group of islands located about twenty miles west of the southern tip of Okinawa, Ryuku Islands, Japan. The harbor where we were anchored was known as Kerama Kaikyo. According to Captain Lally we were the first ammunition ship to anchor in Japanese waters.

The *Stockton* arrived at Kerama Retto that morning and signaled to us that they had sunk the Japanese submarine. Less than two hours after our arrival we were discharging ammunition to LCMs (landing craft, mechanized) for delivery to two aircraft carriers. The next day was the big day, "L Day" at Okinawa.

As Captain Lally said, the next twelve days were a "continuous living nightmare." The men handling the ammunition worked day and night as they passed ammunition to more than sixty ships, including battleships, cruisers, destroyers, aircraft carriers, and LCTs (landing craft, tank). For the men working in the holds it was "four hours on and four hours off" around the clock. We discharged over three thousand tons of ammunition in thirteen days and went to General Quarters thirty-nine times. Orders to go to General Quarters were sent to us via TBS from SOPA (Senior Officer Present Afloat) on the USS Mount McKinley (AGC-7). It meant that an enemy plane had been sighted or that a "bogey," an unidentified aircraft, had been picked up on the radar screen.

We kept sentries posted both at the bow and at the stern of the ship to be on the lookout for unidentified boats or suspicious crafts approaching the ship.

Okinawa and Kerama Retto were approximately 350 miles from Kyushu, one of the four main islands of Japan. The Japanese were now using suicide planes. They were called Kamikaze, which means "divine wind." The kamikaze pilots—many of whom were only 18 or 19 years old—would deliberately crash their aircraft, loaded with bombs, on their targets. During the invasion of Okinawa, massed suicide sorties, called "floating chrysanthemums" by the Japanese, sank 36 ships and landing craft and damaged 368 ships and landing craft. It was estimated that 5,000 kamikaze pilots died. More than 4,900 United States seamen were killed and 4,824 wounded.[7]

April 6, 1945 is another day that none of us on the *Las Vegas Victory* will ever forget. For a 36-hour period during April 6 to April 7, the Japanese sent down from Kyushu to Okinawa and Kerama Retto 355 suicide planes.[8] It was a one-way trip for these Japanese pilots.

Our ship was at anchor and heading in a northerly direction. We had landing crafts tied up to both sides of the ship, receiving ammunition to be delivered to the *USS Tulagi* (CVE-72). At 3:20 PM we went to General Quarters on notice via TBS from SOPA. Although both the Captain and the Executive Officer were on the bridge, my assignment was to serve as Officer of the Deck.

A half hour later we saw a plane in flames fall from the clouds into the sea off our port beam, distant about five miles. Two minutes later we saw another plane in flames crash into the sea, also off our port beam and about five miles away. This plane had been flying low and appeared to have two or three fighter planes on its tail before being splashed. Every pair of eyes peeled the horizon for any signs of enemy aircraft.

On board the ship, working parties helped transfer ammunition to the LCMs. They scrambled to get off the ship, and the LCMs cast off as fast as they could, wanting to distance themselves from us. Around 3:30 PM we observed anti-aircraft fire on our port quarter. We spotted a Japanese plane flying about twenty to thirty feet above the water and heading directly toward our ship at a distance of about three miles. Along with heavy anti-aircraft fire from other ships in Kerama Kaikyo, our five-inch gun on the stern and the three-inch gun on the bow each fired one round, which burst in the path of the plane at an approximate range of 3,500 yards. When the plane was about 3,000 yards from us, it swerved about 45 degrees to its right and crashed into *LST 447* (landing ship, tank) amidships. *LST 447* was underway and heading in a westerly direction. We observed a huge burst of flames on impact.

About three minutes later, off our port quarter, we spotted another plane flying about seventy-five feet above the water and heading in a northwesterly direction, distant about four miles. There was heavy anti-aircraft fire from ships in Kerama Kaikyo and in the anchorage west of us. Our five-inch gun fired six rounds, and our three-inch gun fired nine rounds at this plane. The plane was hit and crashed into the water near Hokaji Shima off our port beam and about two and a half miles away.

The burning LST dropped anchor off our port quarter about three thousand yards away. We observed survivors getting into boats and life rafts. The LCS (landing craft, support), which was tied up to our starboard side, and the LCT, which was tied up to our port quarter, cast off to go over and pick up survivors.

A few minutes later we spotted another Japanese plane flying on an easterly course and heading toward the small island known as Hokaji Shima. The plane was flying below the clouds and was decreasing in altitude. Again there was heavy anti-aircraft fire from ships in Kerama Kaikyo and in the anchorage west of us. The plane appeared to be hit and passed out of our sight behind Hokaji Shima. We observed a huge burst of flames to the west of the island, off our port beam and about two and a half miles away. It was later learned that this plane had made a suicide crash into the bridge of a merchant Victory ship, the *SS Logan Victory*, loaded with ammunition.

We remained at General Quarters stations, and around 6:40 PM we spotted another plane, which was flying low and approaching our ship from dead astern. Our five-inch gun opened fire when the range was about 6,000 yards. Fortunately, we now had a destroyer on our starboard beam and about 500 yards away. The destroyer and other ships in Kerama Kaikyo opened fire. At a distance of about 3,000 yards from us, the plane swerved to its left and headed in a northwesterly direction. Then the plane crashed into the water off our port beam about 2,500 yards away. The plane did not burst into flames and sank immediately. The reason for the plane crashing into the water is conjectural. Probably the pilot was wounded or the plane had some structural damage. Our five-inch gun had fired fourteen rounds, and our three-inch gun had fired three rounds. Our four port 20-millimeter guns had also fired at this plane.

It appeared that our ship was the target.

During the war the Navy would use fictitious names for ships and locations. Right during the middle of the conflict, a talker on the telephone said, "Hot dog, hot dog, this is ketchup." Standing on the bridge, I could see the men who were telephone talkers tell the rest of the gun crews what had been said, and soon all the men were laughing. It eased the tension of the last few hours.

But still the day was not over. About five minutes later we observed another low flying plane approaching SS Hobbs Victory, a merchant ship also loaded with ammunition that was underway on a westerly course, off our port quarter and about four and a half miles away. The plane was too distant for us to open fire. We observed the *SS Hobbs Victory* firing rapidly, but the suicide plane successfully crashed into the after part of its bridge and burst into flames. The ship remained on a westerly course and left the west anchorage in order to get clear of the other burning Victory ship, the *SS Logan Victory*.

Finally, after being at General Quarters for more than four hours, we received orders that we could secure. All of the officers went to the wardroom and sat numb-like at the table. No one really talked, and no one was interested in playing cards. We all felt sad about the LST being hit. LSTs were large landing ships, with a crew of about a hundred. We figured that they were a bunch of guys just like ourselves. It appeared the the plane had been headed for us, but after the plane had been hit, the kamikaze pilot must have decided to swerve to his right and crash into the LST rather than trying to reach our ship.

Both the *Hobbs Victory* and the *Logan Victory* were merchant ships loaded with ammunition. They were privately owned and not part of the Navy. However, each ship had a Naval armed guard unit manning the guns. Both ships were abandoned. They drifted, burning and exploding for over a day, and were finally sunk by gunfire.[9]

On the *Hobbs Victory*, 15 were killed and 3 wounded. On the *Logan Victory*, 16 were killed and 11 wounded. On the *LST 447*, 5 were killed and 17 wounded.[10]

LST 447 continued burning with heavy smoke, salvage operations having been given up. On the following afternoon we witnessed its sinking where anchored.

General Quarters at anchorage on an ammunition ship was different from General Quarters on most ships. For one thing, all of the ships and boats tied up alongside wanted to get away from us as soon as possible. Hence, we had to cast off their lines. Then, when General Quarters ended, the ships and boats would come back alongside, and the lines had to be secured again. Also, every time we went to General Quarters all five hatches had to be closed. Then they were opened again when we received word to secure from General Quarters.

We missed our meals during General Quarters, but the steward mates made sure that we had some apples and plenty of peanut butter sandwiches, wrapped in wax papers. During our long hours on the bridge, apples and peanut butter sandwiches plus some coffee hit the spot.

Those of us on the bridge and topside always felt sorry for the men down below in the engine room during General Quarters. They could hear the guns firing away, but they could not see what was happening. One time during General Quarters a boatswain's mate handling a winch was lowering steel hatch covers on the hatches. A line to one of the hatch covers snapped, and the hatch cover fell on top of the hatch with a "wham." The men in the engine room all jumped to their feet thinking this was the end. It was a terrifying experience at the time, but fortunately, they could joke about the incident at a later time.

We spent another week at Kerama Kaikyo. More of the same— transferring ammo to destroyers and to landing crafts for delivery to aircraft carriers, cruisers, and battleships. And every day we went to General Quarters two, three, or four times.

CHAPTER 9

BACK TO KERAMA RETTO

After two hectic weeks, we received orders to leave Kerama Retto on Friday, April 13. Although we were happy to heave in our anchor, on that same day we received the sad news that President Franklin D. Roosevelt had died. His date of death in the States was April 12, 1945, but for us, being one day ahead—it was already April 13. All the ships lowered their flags to half-mast.

We were off to a new assignment—to rearm baby carriers (CVEs) at sea. The carriers were making air raids on Japan. Two days later we became part of Task Group 50.8, the Logistic Support Group, with the cruiser *USS Detroit* (CL-8) as flagship. The purpose of this task group was to supply at sea fuel, ammunition, aircraft replacement and stores to various units of the fleet. We were in an area southeast of Okinawa, known as East China Sea.

On April 16 the conditions of the sea were favorable for cargo operations, and the *USS Sargent Bay* (CVE-83) came alongside. The two ships, side by side, steamed along at ten knots. We then discharged ammunition to the baby carrier. This had been our first experience at discharging ammunition while underway. It was a difficult operation, as both ships had to maintain the same speed and also maintain the same distance between the two ships. In our first try at this, all went well.

Two days later the *USS Randolph* (CV-15) came close abeam to our port side to receive ammunition. Again we steamed along at ten knots, and the sea was moderate. Then, a couple of days later while still at sea, we transferred ammunition to the *USS Guam* (CB-2) and the *USS Langley* (CVE-27).

On April 21 we received orders to leave the Logistic Support Group and join a group of ships heading back to Ulithi. This group consisted of our ship, six oilers (AOs), and four destroyer escorts for protection.

On April 24 we arrived back at Ulithi to find that the *Las Vegas Victory* was a ghost ship. According to the scuttlebutt, the Navy term for rumor or gossip, our ship had been sunk at Kerama Retto.

We soon learned that the SOPA at Kerama Retto had requested that the *Las Vegas Victory* be returned to Kerama Retto. Hence, we spent the next ten days loading up ammunition, being transferred to us from merchant Victory ships. Then we headed back to Okinawa.

We returned to Kerama Retto on May 10. Again our task force group consisted of four ships: our ship; an oiler, *USS Kasiaskia* (AO-27); destroyer *USS Dewey* (DD-399); and the destroyer that had escorted us the first time, the *Gillespie*. On twilight and night alerts a smoke screen was laid in the harbor. Smoke screens were laid for our ship by two LCVP (landing craft, vehicles and personnel) smoke boats assigned to us by the boat pool, being a group of boats available for general use at the harbor. The men in these boats would place smoke pots in the water around the ship. These pots would emit smoke, and soon the ship would be covered by smoke and invisible to an attacking plane.

This time we were at anchor at Kerama Retto for a period of twenty-one days, from May 10 to May 31. Again it was work around the clock, transferring ammunition and more kamikazes. On orders from SOPA we went to General Quarters forty-two times, one period lasting from 7:00 PM until 4:00 AM the following day. During this three-week period 425 kamikazes had left Kyusu on their one-way trip to Okinawa and Kerama Retto.[11]

On May 13 at 6:45, we went to General Quarters on orders from SOPA. The ship was heading south. About 45 minutes later we observed anti-aircraft fire directly north of us. A smoke screen had been laid in the harbor, but at that time we were completely in the clear. We sighted a Japanese plane approaching the ship from dead astern.

Five of our 20-millimeter guns opened fire, and other ships in Kerama Retto were firing. The plane passed directly overhead at an altitude of approximately 1,000 feet. Standing on the bridge I looked straight up and saw the red balls painted on the wings. We observed many hits, and the plane wavered and appeared to be in difficulty. At 7:40 PM we received word that the plane had crashed into the water about 3,000 yards from us. Our ship claimed credit for a "sure assist" in the destruction of this plane.

United States ships would paint on the outside of the bulkhead of the bridge a small Japanese flag with the red rising sun in the middle for each plane that the ship had shot down. Not being a combat ship, we were proud to have painted on our bridge bulkhead two Japanese flags, as shown in the picture below.

On May 31 we received orders to return to Ulithi. The fighting on Okinawa had been going on for two months and finally was coming to an end. During the second time at Okinawa we had discharged over 2,700 tons of ammunition. Our trip to Ulithi was in a convoy consisting of nine Navy ships, six merchant ships, and two escorts. After a stop at Ulithi we proceeded singly to San Pedro Bay, Leyte Island in the Philippines, where we dropped anchor on June 10.

Executive Officer, Lt. Manuel Vigil, and Captain, Lt. Commander William Lally, on the bridge.

CHAPTER 10

END OF WAR

After five weeks of receiving and discharging ammunition at San Pedro Bay, on July 19 we received orders to proceed to Eniwetok in the Marshall Islands. During the following week we traveled independently, zigzagging most of the way and arriving at Eniwetok on July 26. Eniwetok was to be a principal base on the way to the invasion of the main islands of Japan. We were scheduled to load ammunition for CVEs, the smaller aircraft carriers known as "baby flat-tops," and take part in the projected invasion of Kyushu, the southernmost Japanese island. The Navy had sent to us charts of the bay at Kyushu.

A few days after our arrival at Eniwetok, we learned that the cruiser *USS Indianapolis* (CE-36) had been sunk by a Japanese submarine on July 30 while traveling through the same general area in which we had traveled on our way from San Pedro Bay to Eniwetok.

Although the war in Europe had ended in May, 1945, the end of the war with Japan still seemed to be a long time away. In July, 1945, we thought that the only way war would end would be by actual invasion of the mainland of Japan. Then, in August, 1945, the two atom bombs were dropped and Japan surrendered. We heard about the surrender over the radio at 11:03 AM on August 13—a most happy day on the *Las Vegas Victory*.

For the next twelve weeks in the ship's log I recorded, "Anchored as before." We had no cargo operations. The deck officers tried to keep the deck gang busy by chipping off rust spots on the ship and then painting. We had a movie about every night. During this time we saw about 70 movies. These movies were the best out of Hollywood. We saw the movie "See Here, Private Hargrove," starring Robert Walker and Donna Reed, at least three times. The crew could recite Donna Reed's lines by memory.

Each day we were hoping to receive orders for our return to the States. The crew began referring to the ship as the "Lost Vegas." It was during this time that the Captain received his promotion to Commander, a three-striper, and I received my promotion to Lieutenant, a two-striper.

As Navigator I had two principal responsibilities: plotting the ship's course and writing the ship's logbook. Being at anchor for twelve weeks, I had no courses to plot, and my daily entry in the ship's log was always the same. We officers were still following our watch schedule and standing watches, but all was quiet and peaceful. I spent a lot of time doing "sack duty"—lying on my bunk and reading.

Finally, on November 7, we received the good news. The Navy had made arrangements for all the ammunition ships to return and anchor in Discovery Bay on the Olympic Peninsula, with Port Townsend, Washington, being the nearest town.

After twelve days at sea we arrived at the Straits of Juan de Fuca with the United States on our starboard side and Canada on our port side—a great trip with no zigzagging. It had been almost a year since we had departed from Astoria, Oregon, back in November, 1944. During that time we had been off the ship just a few hours at such places as Mog Mog, Eniwetok, and Leyte.

That day we dropped anchor in Discovery Bay was a great day for all of us. Not only was the war over, but we were back home, safe and sound. A couple of days later, while standing on the bridge, I looked over to see anchored nearby my first ship, the *Pyro*. The *Pyro* had not been back to the States since the day we departed from San Francisco Bay back in November 1943. She had remained as a part of the Seventh Fleet and had gone from Hollandia in New Guinea to Leyte in the Phillipines.

The bus stop at the southern end of Discovery Bay became a busy place. With several ammunition ships at anchor, the sailors and officers were heading to Seattle for liberty. When I boarded the bus on my first liberty, I met six or seven sailors from my division on the *Pyro*. They were surprised to see me. I explained that while preparing for duty on an APA, I had received orders to report to another ammunition ship, the *Las Vegas Victory*. We had a mini-reunion with a lot of laughs on our way to Seattle.

Although we had good food on the two ships on which I had served, we never had any fresh vegetables or milk. On my first liberty to Seattle, another officer and I went to a restaurant, and each of us ordered a large lettuce salad.

On the *Las Vegas Victory* we always had "sick call" every morning at 8:00 AM. If anyone had a physical ailment or needed medical attention, he was to report to the pharmacist mate at that time. While we were overseas, usually five or six shipmates would appear for the sick call. Strangely, on our first morning in the States nobody showed up for sick call. All the ailments and pains had disappeared.

Older officers were leaving the ship, and sailors who had two or three young children were being mustered out of the service. Even though the war was over, we had new officers and sailors coming aboard. The ships had to be manned until being decommissioned.

The Executive Officer had received his orders for discharge the day we arrived. The Captain left the ship for a couple of days, and I discovered that I was the senior officer aboard and in command of the ship. Fortunately, we were at anchor and had no plans to move. However, with officers and members of the crew leaving the ship and new personnel coming aboard, it was a busy time for me.

I received my discharge papers and left the ship on February 4, 1946. The *Las Vegas Victory* went to San Francisco Bay on February 15. After discharging its ammunition to railroad cars at the Naval Magazine, Port Chicago, California, the ship was decommissioned on April 8, having been in the service of the United State Navy for only one and a half years.[12] The *Las Vegas Victory* received one battle star for World War II service.

The *Pyro* was decommissioned on June 12 at Seattle and was sold for scrap in March 1950.[13] Her years of service went all the way back to 1918. The *Pyro* had earned one battle star for her action at

Pearl Harbor. Later, another ammunition ship was named *Pyro* with designation as AE-24. Also, another ammunition ship was named *Nitro* with designation as AE-23.

Ashore at Eniwetok. Left to right; Lt. L. B. Hanigan,
Lt. (j.g.) H. Cook, and Lt. (j.g.) Michael H. Jordan

CHAPTER 11

CAMARADERIE

The camaraderie on both ships was great—much like the Three Musketeers, all for one, one for all. One thing we officers liked about being an officer in the Navy was the fact that each officer knew his assignment. The Gunnery Officer was in charge of the guns and gun crews. The First Lieutenant was in charge of the maintenance of the ship. The Navigator charted the course and kept the ship's log. None of us interfered with another officer's duties, and this contributed to our camaraderie.

On most ships similar in size to the *Las Vegas Victory*, the captain would eat his meals in his cabin by himself. However, Captain Lally chose to eat in the wardroom with the rest of the officers. He enjoyed the comradeship and joviality. In fact, he encouraged each of us to bring a joke to breakfast. It was a great idea. We always started the day with a chuckle.

If you were lonely, you could always go to the wardroom and find someone to talk to. We always knew which men were waiting for mail from home. One fellow would even read to me his letters from home. War united us.

We did not carry any grudges. One day on the *Las Vegas Victory* another officer and I had an argument about something. That evening as he walked past my cabin, he stopped by and continued the argument. Then he left and started walking down the passageway. After he had gone down the passageway for several steps, I heard him stop, turn around, and start to walk back. I knew what he was going to say before he said it. He said, "Cookie, let's forget it." I said, "That's fine with me." We both laughed, and that was the end of it.

When we were at an atoll or other Navy base in the Pacific, our anchorage was usually a few miles from the nearest ship. Whenever an LCT or a destroyer would tie up alongside our ship, it would cast off as soon as it had received its load of ammo. No ship or boat stayed alongside our ship any longer than was necessary. The crew would joke about the fact that nobody wanted to be tied up alongside our ship, but here we were—on board night and day.

On both ships, we did our best to keep the crew in good spirits. For one thing, the "chow" was good, and the officers and crew had the same meals. We always tried to celebrate the holidays with a special dinner.

Many of the crew were young boys right out of high school. With the good food and those four-hour shifts of handling ammunition, many of them were in top physical shape. Being in the South Pacific and often directly under the sun, many of us acquired a deep tan. When they returned home after the war and walked up the front walk to their homes, their mothers probably realized for the first time that their sons were no longer boys.

The library on the *Las Vegas Victory* had been contributed by the citizens of Las Vegas and contained a stack of magazines, including several copies of *Ladies Home Journal* and *Women's Home Companion*. At first we laughed about it and questioned who would want to read these women's magazines. However, during those twelve weeks after the war had ended and we were at anchor at Eniwetok, we were reading anything we could find. And, of course, a game of cards always helped to reduce the boredom.

CHAPTER 12

AFTER THE WAR

After the war I returned to my hometown, Mishawaka, Indiana, and attended the Law School at nearby University of Notre Dame under the G.I. Bill of Rights. It was not easy shifting from the bridge of a ship to the classroom. However, since most of my classmates were also veterans, we all hung in together. I received my law degree in January 1949 and started my practice of law that same year in Mishawaka.

I married Dolly during my last year in law school, and we had three daughters, Nancy, Becky, and Sally. I finally retired from my practice on July 1, 1996.

Probably due to the small size of the crew and the short time that we were together, the *Las Vegas Victory* faded into history. Although some of us kept up a correspondence, we never had a ship reunion. However, the *Las Vegas Review-Journal*, of Las Vegas, Nevada, did run a feature story about the ship in its January 23, 1995 issue.

About eight years after the war had ended I had a surprise reunion with one of my fellow officers from the *Las Vegas Victory*. I was practicing law, with my office in downtown Mishawaka. One day when I had a tight schedule, I decided to walk down to Mark's, a Chinese restaurant located about two blocks from my office and known for its quick service. I climbed onto the stool at the counter and ordered the special lunch for that day. I looked at the man sitting on the stool next to me, and he turned and looked at me. "Cookie!" he shouted. My lunch mate at the counter was John Moss. The two of us had climbed aboard the *Las Vegas* at Astoria that wet and chilly night back in 1944.

He had come to Mishawaka from Milwaukee to make a business call at one of the local manufacturing plants. Since both of us had appointments to meet, we agreed to have dinner together that evening at the Lincoln Highway Inn, a popular restaurant in Mishawaka at that time. What a great reunion we had. With both of us laughing and having such a good time, we had to explain to the waitress what it was all about. She was delighted to sit down and hear some of our stories and join in the laughter. What a coincidence that the two of us would meet again!

The *Pyro*, having a larger crew and having been in service for many years, had several reunions. Largely due to the efforts of Paul P. Simon, one of the ship's cooks, we held our first reunion in 1983 at the Holiday Inn in his hometown of Dubuque, Iowa. Nearly two hundred men from all over the United States attended.

One hot and sunny day back in 1944, when the *Pyro* was at anchor in New Guinea with no cargo operations on schedule, we told the crew to put on their white uniforms and we would take pictures of each division. I had a group picture of the First Division—all fifty-two of us. Before going to the first reunion, I had a local photo shop prepare twenty enlargements of this group picture. Then at the reunion I had the pleasure of passing them out to former members of the First Division.

A woman came up to me and asked if I had a picture of the First Division. After saying that I did, she told me that her husband had been a member of the division, that they had met and married while he was in the Navy, that he was now deceased, and that she had come all the way from the East Coast just to see and visit with his old shipmates. I handed the picture to her. There he was—his sailor hat at an angle and a big smile on his face. She looked at the picture, and tears began running down her cheeks. Both of us just stood there for several minutes in silence. She then thanked me, and at a later time I had the opportunity to visit and laugh with her.

I made it a point to do some table hopping and visit with former members of the crew. It had been almost forty years since I had seen them, and at that time they were a bunch of young men. I found out that one of them was the owner of two service stations in Boston and that another had gone to college under the G.I. Bill of Rights and was a veterinarian in Georgia. We all had a great time trading stories.

Since the first reunion had been a success and well attended, reunions were continued on a biennial basis. My wife, Dolly, and I attended several more of the *Pyro* get-togethers. The 1991 reunion was held at Bremerton, Washington, where the *Pyro* had been commissioned back in 1918. The last reunion we attended was in 1993 at Charleston, South Carolina, where we had the opportunity to go aboard an aircraft carrier and a submarine.

As I mentioned at the beginning, it was an unusual experience to have served as an officer on two ammunition ships during World War II. Although more than sixty years have passed by since the end of World War II, I still keep in touch with some of my old shipmates. A certain kind of kinship exists not only with my old shipmates, but also with all men who have served on or are now serving on ammunition ships of the United States Navy. In fact, an association has been formed known as AE/AOE Sailors Association, AE being the designation for ammunition ships and AOE being the designation for ships that carry both ammunition and oil. A newsletter, *Over the Waves*, is published quarterly.

At the 1987 *Pyro* reunion, I served as toastmaster and gave the following toast at the Saturday night dinner. And, of course, a similar toast could be given for the *Las Vegas Victory* and for all other ammunition ships of the United States Navy.

> Here's a toast to the mighty *Pyro*
> To the skipper and the crew.
> While other ships got many honors
> The *Pyro* received very few.
>
> She carried ammo to the fleet
> Through four long years of war,
> And when the fighting was over
> She was forgotten even more.

The men lived on top the ammo
Enough to blow up a city,
But they laughed and played acey-deucy
And never asked for pity.

The *Pyro* was shoved back in the corner
With no other ships close by,
And nobody wanted to come near her
Only to load up and say "Good-by."

Ole AE-1 had done her job.
They scrapped her and closed the book,
But to the men who served on her
She's still swinging around the hook.

So, after all these many years
A big thank you is overdue.
A toast to the *USS Pyro*
And to her grand ole crew!

At the rostrum at Pyro *reunion (1983)*

END NOTES

1   *Dictionary of America Fighting Ships*, Volume V, 1970.

2   *Dictionary of America Fighting Ships*, Volume V, 1970.

3   *Dictionary of America Fighting Ships*, Volume VI, 1970.

4   *Wall Street Journal*, November 12, 1990.

5   Bernard Rice, *The South Bend Tribune*, April 27, 1997.

6   U.S. Naval Institute Proceedings, February, 1963.

7   *The Oxford Companion to World War II*, pp. 642 and 836.

8   Okinawa, *Touchstone to Victory*, p. 82.

9   *Victory in the Pacific*, 1945, p. 196.

10 *Victory in the Pacific*, 1945, p. 390.

11 *The Divine Wind*, p. 135.

12 *Dictionary of American Fighting Ships*, Volume IV, 1970.

13 *Dictionary of American Fighting Ships*, Volume V, 1970.